WHAT BOOKS PRESS

AN IMPRINT OF

THE GLASS TABLE

COLLECTIVE

LOS ANGELES

ALSO BY ELENA KARINA BYRNE

If This Makes You Nervous (Omnidawn Publishing)
Squander (Omnidawn Publishing)
MASQUE (Tupelo Press)
The Flammable Bird (Zoo Press)

NO, DON'T

ELENA KARINA BYRNE

WHAT
BOOKS
PRESS

LOS ANGELES

Library of Congress Cataloging-in-Publication Data

Names: Byrne, Elena Karina, author.
Title: No, don't / Elena Karina Byrne.
Other titles: No, do not
Description: Los Angeles : What Books Press, [2020] | Summary: "Elena
    Karina Byrne's chapbook, NO, DON'T, offers a restless portrait of
    identity that reflects the shifting terrains of desire and gender, of
    personal loss and punishing empowerment, and of political and cultural
    abuse. -- Provided by publisher.
Identifiers: LCCN 2020026496 | ISBN 9781733378987 (paperback)
Subjects: LCGFT: Poetry.
Classification: LCC PS3602.Y76 N6 2020 | DDC 811/.6--dc23
LC record available at https://lccn.loc.gov/2020026496

Cover art: Gronk, *untitled*, 2020
Book design by Ash Good, www.ashgood.design

What Books Press
363 South Topanga Canyon Boulevard
Topanga, CA 90290

WHATBOOKSPRESS.COM

NO, DON'T

Gratitude to all those at *What Books Press*.

For my inspirational friends, colleagues, my brother
Stephen, and my brilliant, miraculous children who
I love so much: Dylan-Tara & Chloe Karina, and
my stepdaughter, Moonya-Merlin!

Always in memory: Mother & Father,
Elena Karina Canavier & William Scott;
poets Agha Shahid Ali, Galway Kinnell,
Brigit Pegeen Kelly, Kurt Brown & Ralph Angel;
and for my first poetry professor, always-mentor,
friend, and other brother, Thomas Lux.

CONTENTS

I. AT A NOSEBLEED HEIGHT: BEES

II. INSUFFERABLE AS THE FUTURE

No sooner does man discover intelligence than he tries to involve it in his own stupidity.

—Jacques Cousteau

AT A NOSEBLEED
HEIGHT: BEES

DURING THE VIETNAM WAR

. . . only the new-growth grass was wet behind her head & back.

She could feel it and she could smell the grass rising up around her,

saw the whole sky and saw the sky in its *de facto* language

even though she was only seven. The year held out

a bird skull in its opened hand, whole.

Other birds were singing in a French film with no subtitles.

It was black & white. But the sky was definitely blue, an invention

of blue. A vector & hinge & rung of only

blue already there, no matter where you looked.

It took a long time. She looked a long time & in lockstep

pressed the tips of her fingers into the mole-black dirt

between grass blades. Only, this is

the wrong story: she did not doom or injure

any animals but she was restless then & she was

glad she was not safe.

TOMBOY FROM THE ART ROOM

I've always wanted to know if I could make/ love to a boy
I've always known was a woman.
—Natalie Scenters-Zapico

Of overnight windows peeled from paper trees,

        Father's art models' bodies were undressed

and charcoal-cornered. Can you see me riding that Native American horse saddle seat,

desert-out, with only oranges to eat, their white-waxed DDT skin flakes shining like

so many dead fish scales from my fingers, all caught fish bodies left market-home

on ice or on the street

against their own dusk stink? See this child

float twenty feet off the ground, middle passage, film blood running through both

boy & girl, playing lover to myself & so sex-like-unsafe: that dream-first

ransom, tied feeling at the wrist, thigh, ankle & neck place, my open mouth

to kiss, pink water toy of the voice silenced

high above brush-line,— my body, my double other body

        rising in void's tin can gravity, paint bleeding

its teeth, sand from the caul ocean, child from adult

& all reversed: perfect idiomatic, always

in the known & known, cat piss from moan, each

dust-green cactus curt below, the far-off smell of fresh blue paint

& the careless exhale

        of waves as they ravage themselves.

MIND GARDEN, RAIN GARDEN

I have a need to see the painting wet
when no one is looking. God-thought if there was such a thing, forlorn of
weeks reaching for days to ride out onto the Indian Ocean like an equation's
argument of waves in their starched coffin white lace I could finger as they roll pass.
There are hands in the paintings: raised, pointing, folded, reaching, reaching . . . There's
an inlay box intended for my ex-lover's hand, a fever-continuing threshold, weather
balloons like colored severed heads laughing their way up the sky's shifting cake layer's
three miles, withholding a formula for desire. Beside the body & its *skying* figures of
speech: night's wax face mask, captured singing. Try to inhale & again, please. Cough
up cadmium twice, suddenly. Carry this caraway seed page away, fill your sea purse head
with the tiny unborn. Painting, like digging up your garden in the dark isn't spring. Isn't
daddy root, mama foliage breathing for some sun. Isn't spring. Isn't season's measure
for your worth. Whoever told you that lied about what's going to happen next:

WHITE DOLL

The real history of consciousness starts with one's first lie.
—Joseph Brodsky

I lied to the mirror
holding my only Barbie doll by the pink neck,
her fixed eyes open, parents
in the other room.

There was a commotion
of high radioactive-white clouds thirsting above & my
body way down below with dusk hour's inconsolable
light between the furniture.

Somewhere, behind the fish tank
in the first knuckle-blue darkness where doll slept
on the bare floor, you could see my brother kneeling

in the clockwise picture, in the weathervane away place,
see the drowning world there always in mourning,
hurtling itself free from us like endangered bees
from a broken jar. At that point

everyone remained silent in the house, listening to
day & listening to night. I could do anything
& it wouldn't matter, all child, feeling myself

both boy and girl full of fear stories no one told me
to tell, the doll's body, shiny
& insufferable as the future.

EASY RIDER

1969

When tree sunlight was breaking overhead they rode

chopper bikes running cross-country blacktops from
the crosshairs
of home, not scissor-happy, he said. Saturday reaches into Sunday

like a heat argument, like your hand in the "redneck" neighbor's head game

                lattice when no one is looking, or like the freedom-

need to see a painting still wet between a girl's legs in a field of music.

I don't have to

ask for my own freedom but I am

willing to ask

for another's and let it hurt, marry Peter Fonda in this future

embrace. Looking down

              on my own road, paved fast-black and comfortless, I want

something I cannot yet name. But there are men like my brother, these men

who take the sky with them when they sleep,
when they take more drugs.

There are women as I will be, adding up like matches

                              between the teeth, working
on first loneliness, who watch . . .

then that man in the scout truck who feels threatened, buck
shotgun aimed
at the biker who already stole the wind

from him.

IMAGINE A RED CIRCLE HERE

> *And if I say "A rose is red in the dark too" you positively see*
> *this red in the dark before you.*
> —Ludwig Wittgenstein

. . . my hand in
what counts as a domain of money, dark

circle when I say what a family says
counting backwards,
to get themselves from here to memory.

     Or revise that: get on a red train, let

the window throw
its live landscape past you,
its numberless thin blue ball gowns, its trees
a garbled tangle
in your hair, ripped-worn sheets of wet green
piled around your feet like the anxious feeling
you once had as a child

in your grandfather's room, there
to count pennies in a jar. So many mourning
doves could be heard but never seen.
The backyard was stitch-fixed in its dawn window.
The jar of copper stink, heavier than your own head
     if held in the jar, its mouth open
like a dropped death-anchor
under the bed all days to come,—

     or revise that: forget my hand, subtract

the smell of pennies from the sound of birds,
the drowning number of days
given away
in the colorless dark,

OK?

LYNNE'S CAR WASHED VIOLENTLY DOWN, OFF THE CLIFF

for my sister

I take the penny from father's hardwood drawer.

I turn the standing upright penny, its copper head cold, turn
and turn till a small whorl-well of a circle bores into the center
of the brick laid in our fireplace. Brick dust cradle. Thumb place.
This fireplace is wingless and cold. The penny multiplies in swarms.
Nine cloud coffins full of pennies are open and floating as bees float,
looking for my ears. Lynne's car washed violently down off
the cliff. I am too young to drive. Today, all memory ruins
downstream to the bee-swarm, becomes a plea from then till

now and grows reason's garden pulled out at the roots.

There's an ocean treading its own water

to the waist of the coastline, water-skin flexing. I am standing
upright: absent-me in a house full of grief and thievery. Above
the thumb place. I was a child there once, both boy and girl, standing
upright. I turned the penny over on the desert brick, in the fire,
stepped into the cold downstream ruin of bees swarming
in the hard rain's garden. I did not know what I was doing.

It was all made of the same shape and sound down there.

DELIBERATE AS THINKING IS THE RAIN

> *. . . has created the type of autonomous picture, which leads,*
> *without motifs from nature to a completely abstract life form. . .*
> *as a Bach fugue is from a carpet.*
> —Paul Klee

Stepping off the door lintel, down onto the grass as the day closed around us, grass,
rising up inside its own squared green,— she walked backwards, walked backwards,
slow full length of the long lawn to the blue Volkswagen Bug, waved and folded
herself inside where her husband and two children waited. No smell or sound in
memory's stranded interior. I don't think she smiled. Mouth closed, hair loose,
hands, facing Mother and me. Nothing else is moving and the sky is so far, so far
an abstract irrelevance. I stared and stared back for as many years as I could stand
her escaping face in its stages of flowering and deflowering from the frame since it
was the last time time afforded us her face, its pale proof and myth, its core of rain
held off from the picture now black and white beneath us and that full body of trees
remaining years into spine and thigh, into skull, into the lungs, hair flickering out like
reversed candlelight in the river's stir, rain kicking itself back in radio static and dragged
chair, her father's, my father's lynched cry-cough down the hall. She told Mother that
she saw herself buried in a dream in the water years before, her children like pendulums
hung from the singing mast of her own voice. She would go out alone to a class and
wedding, the sky bearing its impatient weight over her and everything that could be a
named there. In its random order the rain would then come that night, hard, flooding on
a year in a place where rain never reigns or raises cars or shapes a silence in its loud
punishment mettle scrawl across its own carnal ambition but would and did and made
moan and cage and bad of it.

SUCH THINGS IN ANIMAL SKIN

You already know what I am not saying. Nostalgia
       is coming back to our neighbors now.
I threw the fake white-haired mouse into the high weeds
next to their fence, felt with my hands the cold leaves like
donkey ears. Years we did not measure time by the beginning
or end of the rain. My sister died because of the rain.
Mole ribs broke in the hard ground, the green canary lungs
were crushed by coal and a threshold torrent of deep sea
anchovies were made where we couldn't see them school.
Her car, near the ocean, slid down a canyon and outside
       mother-years passed over the continental divide
in the private garden stopped by snails and birds of paradise,
mocking birds mocking the grey darkness every summer since.
       I am animal-lost near dead Chinese alligators
unable to run sideways, in whale birth, the rooster's severed
head, blue, rust and red, where I am still a child running in
from the rain with our chickens, their feathers wetting
the polished wood floor behind us.
The roulette table of pill-bugs sinking there in the backyard
       mud came to a slow stop.

COW SONG

for Thomas Lux

I heard them, far off, deep-calling
from behind death's invisible floor door. Their wallow
metronome from the after rain mud was one giant body.

      Arizona's yellow arm length of light all
          the way to my own body standing at the edge
of their field held me. I moved toward them and they
toward me, as if to ask
for something from nothing
               as memory does, each face

dumbfounded— dumb and found by
the timeframe of my own fear, surrounded at dusk.
There was a plastic grocery bag, its ghost cornered
small against a tree, and there was a heavy smell.

      Desolation is equal to contained energy now.
Their bodies slow-approaching toward me, my own body
slow inside their circle without *kulning*.

Kulning is a Swedish song for cows, not one
pillowcase pulled over the head sound. Here, mountains
could be seen from far away. An abandoned physics, a floor door,
my head-call herding me, in-hearing nothing but them.

      Bone for bone's female indicates the curved
          inside of the mouth
when singing is grief alone.
You can't stop shifting no matter how imperceptibly you
move. It sounds like confusion in one direction.

I wanted to tell you this in your absence.
        It sounds like the oak
Thomas, it sounds
like the oak floorboards
        in God's head.

HEADING IN A CAR TOWARD BEING 60

I made my brother take
pictures of my trying to fly. Bird-out of body.
We lived
above the steady heave & shale of ocean.
I was hungry climbing into its repetition of waves.
They moved me fast like a car. I caught

        raw sky.

We always buried our pet birds in
        our yard. Their bodies had wings that needed boxes
            like small rooms to keep them from us. Between

wet dirt & dying
is loss of taste, a family who mastered
            avoidance, mastered flight where

to dream is like waving from inside a car,
            opiate praise of sunlight
in new weeds sprung from a concrete crack
along the framed freeway.

I did not come here
to make sense of who I was. No one
would be able to tell you where I came from,
even if I told you,

        starting over.

All I can say is we flew

        places & came back.

I need an elegy room full of free tropical birds flying.

              I need a color balloon room like the one
that handicapped child in Canada had
on our stay-over. I was a stranger

in his home that smelled of

              bacon & old roses. We,
we were seven-year-olds   but his mind would always tell him
        he was two. Before you

write his future epitaph, remember,

        there was no difference between
us when it came to repeated killing of
the balloons. It was a loud flying away from my body,
confused breaking of color from the room.

We were both so hungry after, and so terrified of each other.

        Remembering this now,
          I am terrified of myself.

NO, DON'T

for the two of me

the thing that eats the heart is mostly heart   and there
I wish, in the burly sun blossom-backwards garden I was hungry,
so damn hungry and afraid again by full-mouth-desire.
Don't   take this as a garroted good-bye, your airless thrive ride.
I alone, fear being alone, far from the blood vocabulary. I wish
I knew where I put my fear sitting in   this childhood past, in
its zoo, sitting on the winding Escher stairs, saying this out loud
to my dead mother, so loud,   a lion's head in the mouth loud
it catches audience breath-for-breath measure making us go
home to say it to the father, down, holding court with outbreak.
You can't hear me say this,   off as an asymmetry cry.
        You too are dead in the circus heart alone
because they really, are all gone, and can't feed you anymore.
You can't sit in the lap, on the headmouth, slow   kneel on the floor;
you can't sit in the cement highchair, sit in this landscape room, see this
come-to-crime test,   be alive here for feeling, or take me
to nothing's sound   past longing with the lion
who won't   eat you, who won't eat me, facing
the animal garden,   shaking his yellow haystack head . . .

AFTERLIFE PARLOR FOR INSECTS

for fear

I didn't say there was a fire in the hunting lodge. I didn't say the color
was, if by feeling, a color. For that sunset when there was none, she
looked & looked for insects under the house. Pledged herself in the blood
seeing, in the foreground sensation, rusting harvest. House-houseboat remained
docked, day-in / day-out, rocking before dusk. Cigarette-orange & red beetles
were the best, shining in their match boxes' caught afterlife, bodies
each a shell of shining disposition. But there was a such-sound, a beetle
song-scratch after its life was stopped, exited from the area, the arena of the ear
& the eastern sea. Tales of trouble. Right then, you know that I'm sitting in
the proximity of insects, a three-parts contained invertebrate frame. But
a frame is a solitary place, a size unclear for bees & silkworms' ghost
silk & honey— a hat full of honey, bare ground burning the feet, a blind cough
of clouds that have me for a sunset here as they earwig their way in so that we just
might listen to the far family house sound of orange rocking away from us,
out of the blow-fly boat & into the hoverfly out-fire!

THE DEVIL'S AUCTION:
TWELVE NIGHTS OF DISCOURAGEMENT

Eliza Blasina photo

You can't put into words, some nights, nightfall,

& night and fall from sleep, going out of business, the girl

given a white horse headdress & costume horse gown, the photo, *entered*

according to Act of Congress in the year of 1867, white tights & hoof shoes

set in sepia against a wall where she might walk out through a stone gate into

 the rough lake, her sexual horse tail waving.

 Who would pay *The Devil's Auction* price for a bad-looking lot

of gorilla hands, tiger rug, ivory netsuke, one wedge-shaped wood tool much

worn, & from inside a man's consciousness, an iron nail, body-saw, gold tooth

& an empty enamel snuff box for the sale price of another night, all sales, final?

Round beads, bells around the ankles. Public domain dance,

 she gallops & gallops, hoof & toe, her head & the horse's head

atop set straight for seeing into the past evidence of temptation to be on the run

 in the night, the horsemeat crowd cheering.

CANNIBAL HOUSE

. . . it's really, really, laborious to reel the silk from spiders.
They are territorial, and they are cannibalistic, so you
can't really house them.
—Dr. Anna Rising

Stronger than steel, spider silk weaves where I can't see or sow, sew the thought
back to its belief, house any religion safe from its painting, or chapel-ask for it,
for your (you meaning me) past, that great hunger unknown warehouse, death-
house or wheelhouse, knitting factory if you have it out for the mind's slave
labor over steeplechase grass. Memory tells you this homeless man tried to drive
away the family car, you still in it. Dad threatened to punch him. But Dad was a
gentle art teacher who wore white shirts. Your older brother says not quite so.
The man lives in the bushes. The medical team had newcomers in for repairs, door
jammed & starved for red paint. Artificial spider silk is now made from bacteria. I
had a fever once, over 104, asked Mother if I could eat the cookie of her coat button.
They sent me to the white hospital. It's the color no one remembers to mention. A man
on drugs once broke into our huge house, hovered at the top of the stairs as I rushed up,
two steps at a time, for my room. Dad chases him down the street, ready to hit him.
The spider fabricated protein's thread is always there for you if you have nerve injury,
fibers from a spinning device like a tiny home. Where there's an unwanted passenger
with us, crash culture's last resort in the printer, its hybrid house strong as steel, plastic
in the gaps. The past can live there too. It's just started, if you keep telling the story to
someone new. Now. My brother had an empty cricket cage, kept me out of his room.
Then. Our half-sister smells like fresh cut grass. Our half-sister slid down a canyon in
her car during a rain slide late at night. Dad looked & looked for her with your older
half-brother. Hyphenated. Half enough to make him look like Dad. You looked out that
spider-feeling window for the memory of your sister. She now lives in the water, in all
sounds of rain when it remembers its own rage hitting the side of the car. Someone's dad,
I only met once, took all of us neighborhood children in his car to get ice cream, far from
our homes. Dad offered to boxer-punch him in the nose as the two stood in a square of
sunlight. We children play backyard hide & seek all the days, hide in the dark bushes
that were full of spiders. Memory tells you dad hit no one. All but one got out alive.
Memory tells you it will eat another memory when left alone. I swear now our house
looks smaller than my head.

INSUFFERABLE AS THE FUTURE

THE FUTURE IS A BEAST PRELUDE

Rhythm is naturally less reliable on the side of the future.
Between yesterday's nothingness and tomorrow's nothingness
there is no symmetry. The future is but a prelude . . .
—Gaston Bachelard

Violence
is commissioned in the instant
        the drinking game
hasn't yet happened. Life after death comes
before wedding rice is thrown over the shoulder
instead of salt. I want to free myself, but can't.
There's an episode called duration
& it is embroidered under the bed
that belongs to daylight.
So let us begin by saying there is
a fact-accident, a continual
horizon lifted on the androgynous voice
of the seagull suffering for food. The hull
        of waves rises & falls whether it is day
or night, yesterday or today, without
permission. But the aim
is nothingness, the motionless hour nothing
is taken from us, meaning future.
"Within the *smiling regret*" of the past
is Baudelaire's cat's eye, yellow-lit
from within. All we have
to do is wait. Metronomic on the lake, I know
a duck hunter's decoy won't sink in the rain.
Dead, Father still
opens the door for Mother in the dream,
        half singing.

ECLOGUE IN HERZOG'S
ORANGE & WHITE

Then *I say Thirst* sitting in a field, after
its orange light falls, drinking five glasses of childhood
milk at a time, as the *train moves . . . moves into fathomless space,*
unwavering, the light staved from LA, Munich to Paris, devoid of
personal instructions. Rain comes. *Rain can leave a person blind*
or in shadow. I wave my hands over my head, two more
hours, as if you were still here. I make amends with desire.
Your distances. Your grief rhythm. An accident

road is covered in salt, mouth in salt, and above the crows'
height of the sky, clouds are stacking their milk paintings.
Look at them. Far off and up close. Look down at
the mother walking over orange beach debris, sorting.
Even the constantly moving water turns orange: Bright

accident. Here, *I prepare a few French sentences.*
For the cigarette I will never smoke. For the entire film
quenched on rain and darkness, implying a smell of oranges
swelling in the white viewing room. *While eating my sandwich,*
I ate one end of my scarf, bleeding its orange into my back. But
it will not keep me warm in this thought.

Because you are not here listening to me as *so close*
once that I think I saw the pilot's face veering away

or my own, veering toward, bending over a glass
of milk and an unpeeled orange resembling fish skin.
Both of us made the ugliest gestures away from the sky.
Something then astonished and ripped open, burst
out, cut and bled for miles like a dell of body-mud ditched
in the endless, dense, wildly fecund ice-grey, and to

myself, a long time ago, it was very hard, so post-haste. So,
I now bow, shout, white-knuckle it in the riddle drug of time
that took away the patience of parents and you. Every day said,
"Walk." But mobility scolds this cold. The cold bites back into
the horizon. Like a mother done and extruded from orange tree,
a father upheld, riding a war plane's ghost updraft, these
quiet botanical of words draining the light, de-assembling
a far sound from the milk pouring down God's ceiling.

I outlawed, for us, that force coming from
 inside my morning, my night, my afternoon, my feet
living out their last season of grief. No two people know
alike. Loss, like a bicycle, is a *greasy soul* wheel out of a dark
cemetery coming towards you, inside, every day. As if
orange *apples pummeled the ground* around us, it turns
out, I walked the whole map's enclosures unending.

WE WERE WASTE & WELTER
THERE IN THE DAY: FACEBOOK

The universe is the ultimate free lunch.
—Alan Guth

Appropriation is the only conversation to have. I   dream the same
wave is breaking over me: aqua alga bloom. Everyone   is watching on
shore, wind lost in its own white music. Or is it white noise? The kind
of machine you   buy so you can't hear your neighbor.   You   know, the one
you   heard through the hedge wall where hungry pigeons were breeding.
Who   can blame your theft for feeling? Come to me dear   thousand friends
I   do not know: I   will share. Cockle & critical mass & tracking our
electrons
from unruly kingdoms of north and south in the black hole's spinning top,
Newton   on the way to the store, with shorthand flurry & fleeing from. . .
America's   imaginative engagement is sex & war, unverifiable claim what
cannot be in the stash cash. Looks like me   in your photo. Looks like a motion
ago was expulsion, dull dish rebrand again. Costume cosmic context in the music
silenced in the bushes. I   don't even know what it sounds like in my own closet
when closed in & alone. Faith here fails its own science, is an art argument
with thrown bread, blood puddings & dining chairs, the petted dead, quicklime,
ocean pollution & a plum for the sleeping eye. Welcome now.   Welcome . . .

PALM SPRINGS,
PALE AS A CHURCH CANDLE

for Darrell Larson

tipping its scales, imaginary
gun in your hand,
your back turned, the road rising
up, mirage-black from the blacktop
and you can't see sundown where
you're going fast to wake up in
the horsehair bed over the edge
of the canyon, and you can't see over
the tequila-wood steering wheel now
small in the distance until that hot road
brings the water as if desert mountains, fallen
politics, last cowboy cactus,
you drive and drive and drive
away from the spit-shining
and lizard skin, every church rock thrown
centuries ago for left shore and holy smell
of her, ghost in a town of ghost-gods driven,
that your cowboy hat flattened
under the pillow until you ran
the hills and in through the shifting
sand shale ghosthouse fields
as giant white windmills would ache
and cut, ache over your head that is now
one starving coyote running,
a nun's habit horizon
disappearing as you near . . .
. . . *Of course the mind is a desert,* Russell Edson said,
one grows use to the simplicity of thirst.

DUMMIES WE ARE

& other such lessons taught
in the classroom, your professor
not telling you
why Hart Crane died, but why
you must drown with him, language
tied around
your ankles and wrists, for a moment
or for eternity, take your pick. Pick
the lock, you can't,
but you can carry a doorknob
into the next life.
After all, you are a dummy
among graduating dummies, some who
never lose the title
because of Descartes' *malin génie,*
evil spirit immune from doubt
who would make him give assent
to the mathematical propositions,
(let's imagine, say, who is likely to die first)
which are in fact false
as the last words you wrote
to end a bad poem about water.
Because tsunami is not a wave
but an act of the god of middle earth,
a hot-headed being in charge of moles,

worms & root knots and ancient dust
carried centuries on the back
of a humpback whale.
Or somebody's god
behaving badly, cleaning
the clocks, cleaning out
the philosophical garage, wiping
the earth's floor
with a few hundred
thousand souls, just so
the dummies can learn something
& the dumb can learn even more.
Yet we are told
we are not stupid, just not ready,
brain in a vat, rat
behind the walls gnawing for his life
& you, you, standing
in a torrential storm
somewhere you don't recognize,
at the side of a dark road looking
for a ride
away from shore, dry pen
in one hand, thumb out
on the other, waiting
for the intelligent answer.

TEMPER TANTRUM IN
THE GARDEN OF GOOD-BYE

Learn to love the paradox. Speak again.
—C.D. Wright

Filling up the water with knives, the Ice Age
came & went, its frozen middle miles of only oyster
beds, opened the body-kingdom

                      in an underwater white rage

as everything slowly died: shiver and timber in
the tambour embroider sound. Now being alone is not the finish

                  line months always repeating themselves

in privacy. Alone: not black galley absence made in the marriage
double ribcage-bed, nor singing the skin's sinking shape asleep. No.
Not the mind's time walkabout, blue & green broken bottles'

                  foliage unfolding out in the street.

      Is not to peer years in the alert direction, or toward
the low-slung opening portal with borrowed joy's live violence
lost, our planet's in-killing battle where common birds might escape

                the fumes' factory mirror cradle mid-breath.

& might each new square measurement rise, rise as updraft
cant-warm, warm & warmer, away from the fish & their green
runway to the vinyl sky with our scream,

              so that the rest of this farewell world

might return biting? What speech, persistent, a rage, self-sufficient,
a self-subsumed face, finds its mouth open, letting go the mind,

                  fly trap for amber.

YOU'RE BEARING: 1619-2019

*The concept of human races began during the
Spanish Inquisition (around 1480)*
—Eliza Sankar-Gorton, *The Huffington Post*

What language are you now? Blood-fuck blank-made

on these leaves, (brother was blood in the ears) blood

      bitter crop, body-doubt, the poplar rain falling grape-grey in

this cricket eating fury again, from someone else's tantrum madness,

the limb tree, berries rolling under the dining table, the untied city rope

hanging, scraping (I dragged myself from yard to yard) knee. Kneel,

& elbow-first on concrete, tire marks on my skin

(they skin animals fur-first)

not mine, but however, mine: inherited & ashamed &

born ass-asleep white with itch root & rot, that (men) will work

      to hate each other a day in their hate

toward someone they don't know, having

their way beneath steeplechase hours, beneath colorless breath

to color (sister slow asleep there) & in the leaves of these

eaten dry crops made all of concrete body, little mouthfuls of

south song, dead salt thrown overboard, that by word

        origins, tongue out & heat-wasted,

such sass, such now, such shame rises in the outcrop's god cotton gut

shout & sweat wheat life fire, me, given against my will, blood genes

apple-split in the subtitle in the peach head

knot of history, sick in this instrument stomach.

AFTER-ELECTION DISPLAY CASE:
I AM THE WALRUS

Treat ourselves to grief
—Camille Rankine

What it was like to be this that boy blue girl,   an event child
of the past "tomboy skinny bones jones" dirty-running naughty
with all the neighborhood kids over stone   walls of every gone
gooseflesh   backyard till dusk, till today-day America died
                                in the inner ear, its death

rattle like fireflies trapped

inside a bottle forgotten under the bed
                        facing the cabinet all year,
taxidermy's world on a leash against inaction?   What downpour-
brawl of business into the city's watched pot crock   can we find
ourselves singing? We people, we brick,   foliage & insect, the who
no one, the elect,   and him, him leering, bleached as from   pig skin
& wheeled-in a glow-gold, for who knows   how long hate had it
coming, his brick dust on the lips, piss-smelling turpentine in
the fake hair on fire?

We lose our own skin in the game,   end of road's end
rope, round tied to the moon's lime face,
so broad it will drag up the drowned boat of us, umbilical-choke
us   in our chain link sleep,   greed-bred brow,
its liar bone stuck in the throat so we can't
                                sing anymore, its white
face broken china on the coin placed
over heart, each eye, over nipple, orifice, — forget your childhood —
goo goo g' joob,   —serviceable villain in office—
in & in he comes . . .

MOUTHPIECE: VOTE

anarchy to the horizon line . . .
—Sylvia Plath

Dear doorstop, dear number outrider.
Dear turnkey phrase, fallen teeth,
I admit fatigue in these syllables
that rise like wine corks in my dry politic Mouth,
creating of sorts, a dull chaos complaint
ghost speech. Mouth,

fall open, you say. Mouth:

Make eggshell rain,
fear the anatomy of nothing, say
what you will without the will's hand on
the brain wheel...
like a driver with her eyes closed,
the car filling with blackberries,
the gravel roads' black tongues out
for blood. Mouth it:

No one is taken care of,
not even stranger sky or family ocean
or the animal-losing species,
so, go ahead, here
in the punishment room timeframe
you did not count on
in the contest, with all that money honey

humming an anthem impatience,
all the punch holes'
eyelet paper snowfall and
etherized light hives' wax on fire,

with unruly language
to make change happen
for other countries, each
far-off ocean's spit and polish
salt and sugar ballad surrender, patriotic
flags of breath against dusk's
rising bruise-blue vernacular...

Mouth, go, go ahead: VOTE

ACKNOWLEDGMENTS

Gratitude to all those at What Books Press!

Much gratitude to the following where these poems originally appeared, sometimes in different form.

Journals & Magazines

"During the Vietnam War," *Poetry*

"Tomboy from the Art Room," *BOMB*

"Mind Garden, Rain Garden," *Poetry*

"Lynne's Car Washed Violently Down, Off the Cliff," *Poetry*

"Deliberate as Thinking Is the Rain," *Plume*

"Such Things in Animal Skin," *Women's Studies: An Interdisciplinary Journal*

"Cow Song," *Poetry*

"Heading in a Car Toward Being 60," *Spillway*

"*No, Don't*," *Academy of American Poets: Poem-a-Day*

"Afterlife Parlor for Insects," *Sand*

"*The Devil's Auction*: Twelve Nights of Discouragement," *Women's Studies: An Interdisciplinary Journal*

"Cannibal House," *diode*

"The Future is a Beast Prelude," *Terminus Magazine*

"Dummies We Are," *Poetry*

"Palm Springs, Pale As A Church Candle" *The San Francisco Chronicle*

"Temper Tantrum in the Garden of Good-Bye," *Poetry International 25/26*

"You're Bearing: 1619-2019," *BOMB*

"After-Election Display Case: I Am The Walrus," *Enchanting Verses*

"Mouthpiece: Vote," *Poetry International 25/26*

Anthologies

"White Doll," *Redondo Poets Anthology; Círculo de Poesía* Anthology, Mexico. The *Círculo de Poesía Anthology* is part of *Inicio* international online magazine, circulodepoesia.com. Thank you to the translators, editor Anthony Siedman, and guest editor Ramón García.

"Easy Rider," *REEL VERSE: Poems About the Movies* (Everyman's Library Pocket Poets, 2019).

"*Imagine a Red Circle Here*," *Eternal Snow: A Worldwide Anthology of One Hundred Poetic Intersections with Himalayan Poet Yuyutsu RD Sharma* (Nirala Publications, 2017).

"Eclogue in Herzog's Orange & White," *The Eloquent Poem: 128 Contemporary Poems and Their Making* (Persea Books, 2019).

"We Were Waste and Welter There in the Day: Facebook," *Republic of Apples Democracy of Oranges: New Eco-Poetry from China and the United States* (University of Hawaii Press, 2019).

"After-Election Display Case: *I Am the Walrus*," *Enchanting Verses: USA Jubilee Edition Anthology* (online edition).

NOTES

"During the Vietnam War"
includes my first memory of being self-aware as a small "human," a conscious participant of an omnipresent universe.

"Tomboy from the Art Room"
This is based on a pre-teen dream I had of flying and of doubling myself —
kissing my *other* selves, as both boy and girl.

"Deliberate as Thinking Is the Rain"
The epigraph comes from this article: https://socialecologies.wordpress.
com/2016/01/29/chasing-the-void-modernity-and-the-abstract/
Paul Klee, speaking of an exhibition by Robert Delaunay, remarked that he
"has created the type of autonomous picture, which leads, without motifs from
nature, to a completely abstract life form. A structure of plastic life, nota bene,
almost as far removed as a Bach fugue is from a carpet." (ibid., p.9)

"Heading in a Car Toward Being 60"
Our first family trip to Europe: the airline, because of a delay, announced an
unexpected overnight stopover in Canada. They placed us in a home rather than
a hotel; the family we stayed with had a mentally handicapped boy my age,
celebrating his seventh birthday. They had filled a room with balloons for us to
pop. I felt it was a strange game but said nothing and played along. That evening,
the boy and I exchanged our talking stuffed animals (each had a pull-cord to
make the animal talk: mine was Bugs-Bunny, his, a Saint Bernard). Despite my
reluctance to make the exchange, I felt sadness for the boy. I have remembered
that moment over the passing years with a mutable understanding of myself.

"'The Devil's Auction': Twelve Nights of Discouragement"
"The Devil's Auction" is the title of a public domain photo; quoted lines also
belong to the photo. This is one of the few times I've written a poem directly
from a photo image. I wish I could find such a costume!

"Cannibal House"
There are some deliberate tense shifts to mimic time's overlap-recall.

"Eclogue in Herzog's Orange & White"
My father, artist and art professor, born in 1908 in Glendale, California, next to
fields of orange groves, ate endless oranges and drank nine glasses of milk a day,
and Mother, who was a painter, twenty years younger, loved all the variations
of the color orange, even had entire dreams in the color orange. The poem was
inspired by Werner Herzog's book *Of Walking in Ice*, a diary of his three-week
pilgrimage from Munich to Paris to "save" his dying friend, fellow filmmaker Lotte
Eisner. I deliberately swerved from Virgil's original concept of the pastoral; nature's
ephemerality of beauty mirrored the underlying human persistence of grief felt in
Herzog's book and in my own life after loss. The intransigent, overriding principle
of this Eclogue arises from an overlapping-interchange of timeframes and voices.
All italicized lines belong to Herzog, which engendered a fresh consciousness for
those stanzas.

"Dummies We Are"
For Thomas Lux, my first freshman poetry professor and my four-year assigned
"Don" at Sarah Lawrence College. In 1978, he jokingly, and with warm fondness,
declared we were all "dummies," his freshman dummies, and would be so until we
graduated. He was a brilliant teacher and one of my dearest friends until he died.
The poem attempts to mimic his tone.

"Temper Tantrum in the Garden of Good-Bye," "You're Bearing: 1619-2019," and
"After-Election Display Case: *I Am the Walrus*:"
These three poems respond to the horrifying, resurging hatred in our country
toward people of color, immigrants, women, gay and trans communities, disdain
for the poor, and on and on—the hatred that is supported, and further incited by
our solipsistic, morally bankrupt, and intellectually feeble President.

ELENA KARINA BRYNE is the author of four books including *If This Makes You Nervous* (Omnidawn Publishing, 2021). She also has a completed collection of "Interrupted Essays": *Voyeur Hour: Meditations on Poetry, Art & Desire*. Elena is a freelance lecturer, editor, Poetry Consultant & Moderator for *The Los Angeles Times* Festival of Books, and the Literary Programs Director for The Ruskin Art Club. A Pushcart Prize recipient, her publications include *Best American Poetry, Poetry, The Paris Review, The Academy of American Poets Poem-A-Day, BOMB, Volt, Denver Quarterly, Verse Daily, Poetry International*, and *The Kyoto Journal, New American Writing, Blackbird*, and *Narrative*, among others.

WHAT
BOOKS
PRESS

LOS ANGELES

WHATBOOKSPRESS.COM